W9-CGN-024

Philippines

by Anne Schraff

Carolrhoda Books, Inc. / Minneapolis

Photo Acknowledgments

Photographs, maps, and artworks are used courtesy of: John Erste, pp. 1, 2—3, 13, 26, 27, 30-31, 33, 35, 36-37, 39, 40-41; © Stephen G. Donaldson, pp. 7 (right), 10, 18, 21 (left); © SuperStock, Inc., pp. 6—7 (top), 24 (both), 25, 28, 29, 30, 32; © Victor Englebert, pp. 8, 9 (left), 17, 20—21 (top), 21 (right), 23, 26, 27, 33, 34 (right), 38, 40, 41, 43, 44; © John Elk III, pp. 9 (right), 12, 13, 34 (left); © Jay Ireland and Georgienne Bradley, p. 11, 14 (right), 22 (both), 31; © Elaine Little/ World Photo Images, pp. 14 (left), 15 (right), 16, 19, 30 (both); Laura Westlund, pp. 5, 15, 25; Philippine Embassy, p. 36; Philippine Department of Tourism, Manila, p. 42. Cover photo of swimming Filipino children by © Elaine Little/World Photo Images.

Carolrhoda Books, Inc.
A division of Lerner Publishing Group
241 First Avenue North
Minneapolis, Minnesota 55401 U.S.A.

Website address: www.lernerbooks.com

Words in **bold type** are explained in a glossary that begins on page 44.

Library of Congress Cataloging-in-Publication Data

Schraff, Anne E.
  Philippines / Anne Schraff.
    p.   cm. — (A ticket to)
  Includes index.
  Summary: Introduces the people, geography, language, customs, lifestyle, religion, and culture of the Philippines.
  ISBN 1-57505-124-9 (lib. bdg. : alk. paper)
1. Philippines—Juvenile literature. [1. Philippines.] I. Title II. Series.
DS655.S472 2001   99—050691
959.9—dc21

Manufactured in the United States of America
2 3 4 5 6 7 — JR — 07 06 05 04 03 02

Contents

Welcome!	4		Festival Time	28
Land	6		Small Talk	30
Earth Movers	8		School Days	32
In the Tropics	10		Rice Is Nice	34
First Folks	12		Tell a Story	36
Filipinos	14		Art to Use	38
Family Time	16		Move Your Feet	40
Busy Manila	18		Fun Stuff	42
Country Life	20		*New Words to Learn*	*44*
Dress Up	22		*New Words to Say*	*46*
Getting There	24		*More Books to Read*	*47*
Off to Church	26		*New Words to Find*	*48*

Welcome!

The Philippines is a chain of more than 7,000 islands scattered across the Pacific Ocean. Located just south of the **continent** of Asia, the Philippines are washed by the Philippine Sea to the east. The South China Sea splashes between the Philippines and Vietnam to the west. In the southwest, the Sulu Sea separates the Philippines from Malaysia. The Celebes Sea lies between the Philippines and Indonesia.

How Big?

If you were to squeeze all of the Philippine islands together into one big landmass, you would have a country about the size of Italy or the state of Nevada.

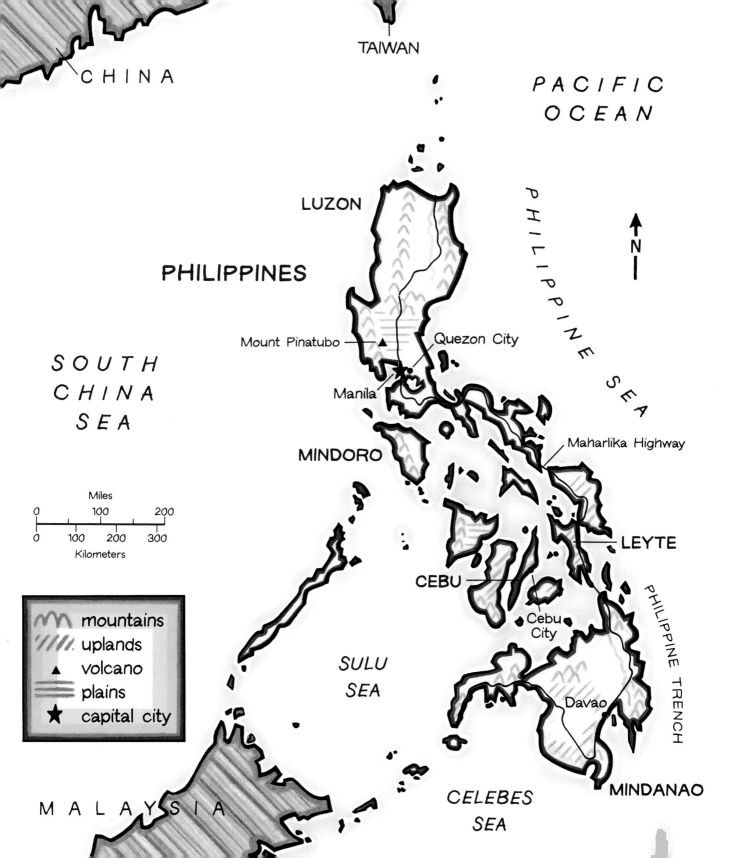

TAIWAN

CHINA

PACIFIC OCEAN

PHILIPPINES

LUZON

N

SOUTH CHINA SEA

PHILIPPINE SEA

Mount Pinatubo ▲

Quezon City

Manila ★

MINDORO

Maharlika Highway

Miles
0   100   200

0   100   200   300
Kilometers

LEYTE

CEBU

Cebu City

PHILIPPINE TRENCH

∿ mountains
/// uplands
▲ volcano
≡ plains
★ capital city

SULU SEA

Davao

MINDANAO

MALAYSIA

CELEBES SEA

Land

The sandy beaches in the Philippines (above) *are a fun place to catch some sun. Then cool off in this blue lagoon* (facing page) *on Coron Island.*

Sandy beaches ring many of the islands. Farther inland you might find steep mountains or gentle hills. In other areas, lush **tropical rain forests** blanket the landscape. Some of the islands are so tiny that no one lives on them. But others, such as Luzon, are huge! Manila, the capital of the Philippines, lies on the island of Luzon.

Map Whiz Quiz

Take a look at the map on page 5. Trace the outline of the Philippines onto a piece of paper. Can you find the South China Sea? Label it with a "W" for west. How about the Philippine Sea? Mark it with an "E" for east. Search for the island of Taiwan. Label it with an "N" for north. Use a blue crayon to color in the seas that surround the islands.

Earth Movers

Millions of years ago, **volcanoes** and **earthquakes** worked together to push the Philippines above the surface of the

Pacific Ocean.

These days small earthquakes shake the islands at least five times each year.

The island of Luzon has both volcanoes and rice fields (facing page). *Earthquakes have damaged this building in Baguio, on Luzon* (above). *Residents of this village near Legaspi, on Luzon, live in the shadow of a volcano* (left).

In the Tropics

The Philippines lie in the **tropic zone,** so daytime temperatures reach 80 degrees for most of the year. During the rainy season, which lasts from May through

During the rainy season, rivers rise and waterfalls rush down the hillsides.

November, winds blow rain clouds over the islands. The rainwater helps the Philippines' rain forests stay green and thick. Plants such as bamboo, papaya, banana, cassava, and pineapple thrive.

Spinning Heads

In the Philippine rain forests, you might spot a tarsier. This **nocturnal** animal is related to the monkey. It has huge eyes and frog-like legs. Its hands are like a monkey's, and its coat is a silky grayish brown. The tarsier can spin its head halfway around on its neck. Yikes!

First Folks

Mountain tribe homes have been re-created at the Bontoc Museum in Mountain province to show visitors how residents of the Philippines lived long ago.

As long as 30,000 years ago, people from the Aeta **ethnic group** lived in the Philippines. The Aetas may have walked across land that connected the Philippines to

Following the Stars

Malay sailors found their way to the Philippines by watching for changes in the clouds, stars, and ocean waves.

southeastern Asia. After the Philippines became islands, members of the Malay ethnic group arrived from Southeast Asia in canoes. In northern Luzon, the early Malay grew rice.

Archaeologists discovered these ancient coffins in Matagkib Cave in Mountain province.

Filipinos

Filipinos (left), *Ifugaos* (above), *and Muslims* (facing page) *make the Philippines their home.*

People who live in the Philippines are called Filipinos. Most Filipinos are from the Malay ethnic group. Other Filipinos belong to one of 80 other ethnic groups.

The Tagalogs, a Malay people, are the largest

group in the country. Most Tagalogs live in the Manila area. In the mountains of northern Luzon, members of the Aeta,

Bontoc, and Ifugao ethnic groups farm rice.

The Philippines' flag has been used since 1898.

Family Time

How many people live together in your family? Filipino households are usually pretty big. Grandparents, parents, children, and even cousins and aunts live together in a **compound,** a group of houses built close together. The houses are small. Most kids

Would you like to live in a compound with your parents and grandparents, like this family in Zamboanga?

share bedrooms with their brothers or sisters.

In the typical Filipino family, the father goes to work every day and is the head of the family. Moms pay bills, shop, and cook.

Many Filipino families like to gather on the beach for a barbecue.

Pakikisama

Mothers teach their children the custom of *pakikisama*. Pakikisama is a way of showing kindness and consideration to others at all times. Filipino kids learn from a young age not to yell at a store clerk for making a mistake or not to make fun of a schoolmate.

Busy Manila

Modern Manila has skyscrapers and palm trees.

In Manila, people and cars crowd the streets. Manila has lots of towering skyscrapers and brand-new shopping centers. Some city dwellers own televisions, computers, radios, and telephones. They live in new

houses and drive zippy new cars. But in poor areas, families live in rickety shacks made of metal and cardboard. They work hard just to make enough money to buy food.

Country Life

Farmers use water buffalo, or carabao, to till their rice fields.

Most Filipinos who live in the countryside are rice farmers. People have carved shelves of land, called terraces, into the hillsides and mountain slopes. Farmers plant rice in the wet, flat terraces. The whole family helps plant, harvest, and then sell the rice at roadside stands.

Many families build their homes on stilts to keep things dry during the rainy season.

Some Filipinos build their homes on stilts (left) *to avoid floating away during the rainy season. Vivid, green rice fields surround a small Ifugao village on Luzon* (above).

Dress Up

Some men wear barong tagalogs, or embroidered shirts, to dress up (below). This Ifugao family (right) shows off their colorful sarongs, long pieces of cloth that wrap around the waist.

If you are packing for the Philippines, do not forget your jeans and T-shirts. That is what most kids wear.

In the countryside, women might wear *sayas*—long skirts. Men sometimes wear a *barong tagalog*, an embroidered shirt.

Most kids in the Philippines dress in jeans and T-shirts.

Getting There

Make way for jeepneys, old jeeps that Filipinos have made into taxis. Cars, trucks, buses, and bicyclists share the busy streets.

Sailboats (above) *and colorful jeepneys* (right) *are two great ways to travel throughout the Philippines.*

In Manila, catch a ride on the Metro Manila Light Rail Transit. It runs on a track built over the streets.

Take a carabao for a ride!

In the countryside, lots of people walk or hitch a ride on a water buffalo.

Dear Cousin Jamal,

The Philippines is such a fun place! Yesterday I swam in the South China Sea and picked ripe bananas. I just took my first ride through Manila on a jeepney. Wow! A jeepney is like a taxicab, but the drivers decorate them with miniature horses, bright tassles, or anything they can think of.

See you soon,
Marcus

Sum Mainetha
Waum Kaillim
Thalumhu, Simlu
730n, Laurathu

Off to Church

Most Filipinos are Roman Catholic. During **Lent,** Filipino Catholic communities put on a *sinakula,* a play that tells the story of Jesus' walk to his death. On Easter Sunday, Filipinos go to Mass (church service) to celebrate renewed

On holidays, Roman Catholic kids march in parades (facing page) *that celebrate Catholic saints. During a prayer meeting, Manila's Rizal Park* (left) *fills up with Catholics.*

life. Every region and city has a patron saint, and each year towns host huge celebrations to honor their saints.

Toss a Stone

Muslim families enjoy the Hari Poasa holiday. They fast during the days in the month of Ramadan, then they feast afterwards. At a special ceremony called Panulak Bala, everyone gathers on a beach. A holy man splashes the worshippers with water to represent the cleansing of body and soul. The people cast stones into the water to symbolize the casting off of evil in their heart.

Festival Time

Filipinos who live in Quezon City's Lucban neighborhood celebrate San Isidro Day on May 15. Festivities honor the carabao and give thanks for a good harvest.

Early on the morning of the festival, carabao owners use oil to shine the horns and hooves of their

Filipino girls sometimes string their hair with bright beads for festivals.

animals. Families decorate carts with paper flowers. In the afternoon, the carabaos pull the fancy carts into town.

San Isidro Day honors the hard-working carabao (above). Filipino women (left) in traditional costumes dance in a parade.

Small Talk

Magandang

In the Philippines, people speak more than 80 different languages! Pilipino, a language

Kids learn to smile before they say a word (above).
(Left) *Say Cheese!*

based on Tagalog, is one of the country's official languages. English is the other. Everyone learns Pilipino in elementary school.

Half of all Filipinos speak English and can read and write in English and Pilipino.

Young Filipinos learn whatever language their parents speak.

Umaga po

Body Talk

Filipinos use more than just words to talk to each other. Raising the eyebrows for a moment is one way to say hello. A smile may mean someone is happy, but it may also mean that the person is trying to be friendly.

Pay attention! There is a good chance this lecture will be covered on next week's exam.

School Days

Filipino kids study math, science, Pilipino, English, history, government, and civics. Most schools have gardens where kids can learn how to farm. Kids work hard to get good grades. That means doing homework and taking lots of tests. Teachers post grades for all the school to see. Yikes! Many families throw a big party for kids who earn high grades.

Most students wear uniforms, even those who go to college.

Rice Is Nice

For a Filipino meal, try kabobs, tofu, and vegetables with rice (above). With all of the fresh fruit available in the Philippines (left), Filipinos have no trouble satisfying a sweet tooth.

Polvoron—powdered milk candy—is a favorite treat.

Filipinos eat rice most every day. For a great snack, Filipinos choose sticky rice cakes or *suman,* rice cakes wrapped in coconut or banana leaves. The most popular Filipino meal is *adobo,* a stew of pork or chicken. If you are looking for something sweet, try *halo-halo,* a tasty dessert of fruit chunks, ice, and gelatin.

Dr. José P. Rizal was a writer who pushed for Filipino independence from the Spanish.

Tell a Story

In the mood to hear a good story? In the Philippines, popular **folktales** from Malayan, Chinese, Indian, and Muslim cultures have been passed down through families over many years. Most Filipino folktales teach lessons about life. The story "The Ape and the Firefly," for example, teaches that even people who may appear small and weak can use a little brainpower to win fights.

The Ape and the Firefly

A firefly flew past a big ape one night. The ape asked the firefly why he had a little light. "To scare off mosquitoes," said the firefly. The ape laughed and said, "What a big coward you are to fear mosquitoes!"

"I'm not a coward," said the firefly. "I can beat you anytime." The ape laughed so hard he almost fell down. But then the ape stood straight and tall, waiting for the firefly to try to attack him. The firefly flew up and settled on the ape's nose. To squash the firefly, the ape clamped his hand on his nose so hard that he knocked himself out. The firefly laughed. Just before the ape's hand reached his nose, the clever firefly had flown away. Ever since that day, apes have been afraid of fireflies.

This weaver makes cloth from banana tree fibers called abaca.

Art to Use

Have you ever sat on a work of art? Filipino wood-carvers fashion furniture from Philippine trees. Artists in the town of Betis are known for making the best furniture in the country. Weavers use thread, grasses, and even tree bark to make wall hangings or clothing. On the islands of Mindanao and Mindoro, basketmaking is the thing to do. Artists use bamboo vine to make baskets in many different shapes, sizes, and designs.

Sweet Dreams

Mat makers weave brown sleeping mats from soft, sweet-smelling **pandanus** grass. Filipinos claim that they have the best dreams when sleeping on a fragrant mat. Eventually, the mats lose their scent. No matter—Filipinos just buy new mats at the market.

Move Your Feet

Filipino kids like to hang out and make music with friends.

The *tinikling*, a dance performed on Leyte Island, is fun to watch. Two people hold the ends of two bamboo poles. They clink the poles together in time to the music. A dancer hops between the moving poles.

In the *binusian*, dancers balance jars that hold lit candles. The jars sit on their heads and on their outstretched hands. The music starts out slowly, but soon the pace quickens and the dancers scramble to keep the beat and to keep the candles lit.

These schoolgirls from Leyte Island have to move their feet fast to jump rope.

Fun Stuff

Looking for fun? Go fly a *boka-boka.* A boka-boka is a small, square kite that kids make out of sticks and paper.

Filipinos make a game out of grabbing for fruit. Don't drop it!

Cockfights, or battles between two roosters, are a popular sport in the Philippines.

Or try playing a game called *luksong tinik.* Two kids hold up a long stick while another player tries to jump over it. The kids keep raising the height of the stick until the jumpers can no longer make it. The kid who jumps the stick in the highest position wins the game.

Pile on! If you visit the Philippines, you can cruise around Luzon Island on a cart like these kids.

New Words to Learn

compound: A group of homes with a fenced or walled yard.

continent: Any one of seven large areas of land. The continents are Africa, Antarctica, Asia, Australia, Europe, North America, and South America.

earthquake: The shaking of the ground caused by shifting of underground rock.

ethnic group: A group of people with many things in common, such as language, religion, and customs.

folktale: A story told by word of mouth from grandparent to parent to child. Many folktales explain where an ethnic group came from or how the world began.

Lent: The month before Easter when Christians fast and say they are sorry.

nocturnal: Active during the night.

tropical rain forest: A thick, green forest that gets lots of rain every year.

tropic zone: An area with temperatures high enough for plants to grow year-round.

volcano: An opening in the earth's surface through which hot, melted rock and gases shoots up. Volcano can also mean the hill or mountain of ash and rock that builds up around the opening.

New Words to Say

Aetas	AHY-tahs
barong tagalog	bah-RONG tuh-GAH-log
binusian	bih-NOO-see-ahn
carabao	KAH-ra-bahw
Cebu	SEE-boo
Celebes Sea	SEHL-eh-beez SEE
Filipinos	fihl-ih-PEE-nohs
Ifugao	ee-foo-GAHW
luksong tinik	luhk-SONG tih-NIHK
Mindanao	mihn-da-NAH-oh
Mindoro	mihn-DOR-oh
pakikisama	pah-kih-kee-SAH-ma
pandanus	pahn-DAHN-oos
Philippines	FIHL-uh-peenz
Pilipino	pihl-uh-PEE-noh
sinakulo	see-NAH-koo-loh
Tagalog	tuh-GAH-log
tinikling	tih-NIHK-ling

More Books to Read

Aruego, José, and Ariane Dewey. *Rockabye Crocodile.* New York: Greenwillow Books, 1988.

Dooley, Norah. *Everybody Cooks Rice.* Minneapolis: Carolrhoda Books, Inc., 1991.

Enderlein, Cheryl L. *Christmas in the Philippines.* New York: Hilltop Books, 1998.

Johnson, Sylvia A. *Rice.* Minneapolis: Lerner Publications Company, 1985.

Kinkade, Sheila. *Children of the Philippines.* Minneapolis: Carolrhoda Books, Inc., 1996.

Lepthien, Emily. *A New True Book: The Philippines.* Chicago: Children's Press, Inc., 1993.

New Words to Find

animals, 20-29
art, 38-39

beaches, 6

cities, 18-19
climate, 10-11
clothes, 22-23

dances, 40-41

earthquakes, 9
ethnic groups, 12-13, 14-15

faiths, 26-27
families, 16-17
farmers, 20-21
festivals, 26-27
flag, 15
folktales, 36-37
food, 34-35, 44

games, 42-43

history, 12-13, 14-15
holidays, 26-27, 28-29
houses, 16, 19, 20-21

jobs, 18-19

languages, 30-31

map, 5
markets, 34-35, 44
mountains, 6-7, 8-9
music, 40-41

Pacific Ocean, 4
people, 12-13

rain, 20
rain forests, 6
rice, 34

school, 32-33
seas, 4
stories, 36-37